Twenty-five Years
in the Fourth Grade

Twenty-five Years in the Fourth Grade

Reflections of a Sunday Schoolteacher

Joseph L. Borowitz

Copyright © 2019 by Joseph L. Borowitz.

ISBN 10: 1642540951
ISBN-13: 9781642540956

All rights reserved. No part of this book may be reproduced or transmitted in any form or by any means, electronic or mechanical, including photocopying, recording, or by any information storage and retrieval system, without permission in writing from the copyright owner.

This book was printed in the United States of America.

Twenty-five Years in the Fourth Grade

Reflections of a Sunday Schoolteacher

Joseph L. Borowitz

Copyright © 2019 by Joseph L. Borowitz.

ISBN 10: 1642540951
ISBN-13: 9781642540956

All rights reserved. No part of this book may be reproduced or transmitted in any form or by any means, electronic or mechanical, including photocopying, recording, or by any information storage and retrieval system, without permission in writing from the copyright owner.

This book was printed in the United States of America.

Contents

Preface 9

Chapter 1	Importance of Fourth-Grade Sunday School 13
Chapter 2	Prerequisites for Being a Sunday Schoolteacher 17
Chapter 3	Nature of Fourth Grade Sunday Schoolteachers 20
Chapter 4	How to Conduct a Fourth Grade Sunday School Class 23
Chapter 5	True Stories of How God Works in People's Lives 30
Chapter 6	Characteristics of Students in Fourth Grade Sunday School 36
Chapter 7	Role of the Holy Spirit in Fourth Grade Sunday School 40
Chapter 8	The Role of God-Oriented Wisdom in Teaching Sunday School 42
Chapter 9	Each Class Has a Different Personality 45
Chapter 10	Factors Affecting Our Sunday School Classes 47
Chapter 11	Chain of Command 49
Chapter 12	Westville Prison Visit 56
Chapter 13	Personal Benefits of Teaching Fourth Grade Sunday School 63
Chapter 14	Conclusion 67

Acknowledgement

Blessed Sacrament Church has had two pastors over the last 25 years, Father David Douglas and Father David Buckles. For their spiritual direction and support, the author is deeply grateful.

Preface

The following article appeared in our *Blessed Sacrament Newsletter* of February 2006. It was written by Janine Reklaitis, a fine Christian woman and longtime member of Blessed Sacrament Parish in West Lafayette, IN.

Professor Joseph Borowitz has been teaching the CCD class to fourth graders at Blessed Sacrament for twenty one years now. On December 18 at 9:10 AM I joined the 12 students in his class along with Ashley Rodarmel, his high school aide, for a very inspiring session. Below, I give a glimpse into what transpired that Sunday morning.

First a brief introduction to "Dr. Joe" himself through the questions he answered for me.

What do you teach at Purdue and how long have you been doing so?

For 36 years I have been teaching Pharmacology, the study of drugs, to Pharmacy and Medical students at Purdue.

What motivated you to start teaching CCD and keeps you doing so even with your busy schedule at Purdue University?

I wanted to share with the kids what I've learned about Christ. It was time I started giving actively and being part of God's kingdom here on earth. Like St. Paul, I would feel guilty if I did not share my experiences with others.

Do you see similarities or differences between your current CCD students and those of a decade ago?

CCD students today may be more serious and more in need of a good basic foundation in Christianity than students of 10 years ago. Maybe it's due to 9/11.

What role/responsibilities do parents have in religious formation of their children?

Parents are key players in the CCD Program. They are the first teachers. Also I invite one of the parents to be present in our class each week to read stories to the kids. They see first hand what goes on.

What can the students themselves do to make "Sunday School" a more meaningful, and enjoyable experience for all?

Children who are supportive of the purpose of the class, to make the resurrected Jesus more real in each of our lives, are the most fun to have in class. One memorable moment stands out. We were talking about how Jesus, the Creator of the world, humbled Himself and washed His apostles feet. I commented how amazing this was. One little girl said "Isn't that what He's supposed to do?" How right she was.

Any final comments?

CCD is serious business in this day and age of terrorism, war and economic problems and other difficulties. It is important that the kids know that Jesus rose from the dead and is with each one of us, loves us, cares for us and came to bring us fullness of life. Each CCD class needs to bring the students closer to their Creator and best friend.

Indeed, every week Professor Joe tries to portray Jesus as the children's best friend. To get to know Our Lord, Joe typically starts class by having his students find and write out a verse of Scripture. This is very effective for learning to love the Bible! Class starts with a prayer of Thanksgiving: for the kids, for their parents, for the blessings in their lives. Since this was the last class before Christmas break, pens and candy canes were given to each child and then the class got into the spirit of merriment and traded a few jokes. The main feature was a short video on the Birth of Jesus. Before the video started, what else, snacks were passed around. By now, everyone was truly enjoying theirself. When the talking centered around the Holy Family, one of the children said: "Families will always love you no matter if you make mistakes or sin." Dr. Joe asked: "Do you think that's the kind of love God has for you?" Everyone replied with a loud YES! As the laughter and learning came to a close, another tradition followed. For the ending of the class, the children get to hear a story read by the visiting parent about miracles that happen every day.

This time the privilege was mine. Just before the class ended, I caught one of the happy kids, Corina Almonza, and asked her what she likes about these classes? Without skipping a beat, she shouted out, "They're good: I like my teachers and my friends!"

Chapter 1

Importance of Fourth-Grade Sunday School

Education is not the filling of a pail, it is the lighting of a fire.

—W. B. Yeats

What a challenge it is to make ten—and eleven-year-old children aware of the rich traditions of two thousand years of Christianity and of the powerful, life-giving message of Jesus Christ. Many come into the fourth grade with only a superficial awareness of the whole concept and with many doubts and frustrations. In other words, they are just like adults. Some don't fully believe in God. Some believe in Him but think He really doesn't know what's going on, and even if He did He couldn't do anything about it anyway. The primary task of the Sunday schoolteacher is to reflect the reality of the Living God and to encourage the students to believe in their hearts, not just with their minds. What the world needs in this twenty-first century is effective Sunday schoolteachers, people who can make God alive to young children and make His goodness evident in their surroundings.

Children are the future of our communities and of our churches. If we are to make progress as a society, we need to train our young people in godly ways so that they will be people of faith. Like the rest of us, they have to decide whether to become righteous people or to follow the ways of the world with its bitterness, un-forgiveness, covetousness, and indifference.

In this world of confusion, problems, and strife, we all need the intimate, constant help of our God. Sometimes we live in a sea of imperfection even within ourselves despite our efforts to do good. "There is none that does good, no not one" (Ps. 1:2). Someone once said that a sequel should be written to the book *I'm OK, You're OK* and entitle it *I'm a Jerk, You're a Jerk*. We are all tempted to do wrong things despite our good intentions. "Who is righteous but our God?" (Isa. 45:21). He is someone we can each turn to anytime in this troubled existence of ours. Fourth graders need to know they too can find forgiveness and a refuge in our loving God and receive the comfort, understanding, strength, and peace they need to continue on the narrow way.

Using "Star Wars" jargon, the Sunday schoolteacher is like a Jedi Knight, a spiritual warrior, trying to recruit other Knights in a struggle against evil forces in our part of the galaxy. There's no room for faint hearts in this epic Star Wars episode. We need people of courage and vision who have deep beliefs, who know the power of "the Force," people who will unlock the doors of the upper room and step outside to fearlessly proclaim the life-giving message despite the threat of persecution or even crucifixion. Strong forces of darkness surround us. Bastions of virtue, honesty, integrity, and righteousness are being overwhelmed. We look to our young people to save us as a civilization. But these young Knights need to be mentored by competent elders, to be trained, disciplined, and focused so that they can be effective in combating the evil which seeks to destroy us.

Sunday school children are mostly like the rest of us, struggling to do well despite many problems. There's the bully down the street, chores to do at home, competition for a spot on the little league team, homework nearly every night, etc. So many are from broken homes, and even those families which are intact sometimes don't provide help and encouragement. Sunday school can offer vital support to ten—to eleven-year-old children. They are not too young to understand that we have a God who can provide needed help. Many times there is no one else but God who can really understand us and give us what we need.

Little children have a vague idea that there are different denominations like Jews, Catholics, Protestants, Muslims, Buddhists, etc., but they learn a lot by the time they are in the fourth grade. Elkind[1] distinguishes three stages of child development in attainment of religious identity. At ages

---

[1] David Elkind, *The Child and Society: Essays in Applied Child Development*, Oxford University Press, New York, 1979.

five to seven, children confuse religious denomination with nationality. For example, some think you can't be Catholic and American at the same time. Children at the second stage (seven to nine years) associate behavior with different denominations, i.e., a Jew goes to the Temple or Hebrew school. At this age, they understand an American can attend the Catholic Church. At the third stage (ten to twelve years), they demonstrate an abstract concept of religious denominations and no longer define them by activities but rather according to belief and understanding, such as a Jew believes in one God but not in the New Testament. Grade four Sunday schoolteachers have an opportunity to build on that new awareness and to make the kids feel good about their own denomination without condemning other approaches to God.

For American Catholics, it is especially important to distinguish between denominations and clarify the position of the Catholic Church among the major religions. A statement in the Congressional Record by a congressman from California[2] indicates that there is more prejudice against the Catholic Church in the United States than against any other minority (women, African Americans, Asians, etc.). The historian Arthur Schlesinger Sr. once observed that anti-Catholicism is the most deeply rooted prejudice in the history of the United States. So, if you are in a Catholic Sunday school program ("CCD," Confraternity of Christian Doctrine), you need to assure the students that the Catholic Church is in full accord with all the gospel promises and that no one has a monopoly on the Holy Spirit.

Another important result of Sunday school is enhancement of family spirituality and relationships. Children bring home the stories discussed in school, and interaction with parents in homework assignments promotes a godly orientation in the family. Teachers should be aware that they are not only exposing the children to the love, joy, and care provided by the "Good Shepherd" but strengthening family ties as well.

Finally, the Sunday school program brings together several adults of the parish and binds them together in a common purpose. Some cooperative working relationships develop and some friendships as well. In our parish, we have monthly teachers' meetings which are generally well done and informative regarding upcoming events and projects in which all classes participate. Sometimes it's difficult to be relevant to the

---

[2] Robert K. Dornan, October 19, 1990, H.10684.

actual classroom experience since there are so many different styles of teaching and so many different grade levels. Overall, the Sunday school program does bring people together and is healthy in a spiritual and social sense for the whole parish.

Chapter 2

Prerequisites for Being a Sunday Schoolteacher

The Holy Spirit is the secret of our sanctification. Let us dwell in His powerful, intimate, transforming presence.

—Pope John Paul II, Rome 1998

Most importantly, a fourth grade Sunday schoolteacher should be a deep believer, a person of conviction who has a personal relationship with the Living God and one who has made the effort to understand the mysteries of God.[3] One who realizes that God is aware of what each of us is going through. One who knows our loving God is powerful and He can perform miracles. When I first started teaching Sunday school, I naively thought the children would automatically share my deep convictions and enter into the spirit of the moment when I prayed spontaneously. I was disappointed when they began poking one another during my serious prayer time. So, a Sunday schoolteacher not only must have deep convictions, but also be able to translate those convictions so that a ten-year-old can understand.

In Galatians 5:22, St. Paul gives other characteristics of a fourth grade Sunday schoolteacher. He calls them the "Fruit of the Spirit": love, joy, peace, patience, long-suffering, kindness, goodness, faithfulness, and

---

[3] J. D. White, *Seven Secrets of Successful Catechists*, Our Sunday Visitor Publishing Division, Huntington, IN, 2002.

self-control. Obviously these are fine attributes of someone conducting a Sunday school class.

Many classes tend to act up at the beginning of the fall semester since they come after a carefree summer of fun, and then it's back to work. A high school math teacher told me he also experienced some misbehavior at the beginning of the school year, but despite that you have to keep going and keep giving good lessons. Usually, then they settle down. So, teachers, be prepared. Don't be discouraged and keep doing your best.

In some fourth grade classes, conflicts are in progress. The Sunday school room can be a place where your love, joy, peace, and patience are desperately needed. In one of my classes, a problem had existed for some years, but no one had adequately informed me. In our first session, one little boy refused to come into the room. He said he'd rather just stand outside the door out in the hall. I finally convinced him to at least come in and have a seat in the back of the room. As time wore on, I was the one who didn't want to come into the room.

Later in the semester, I had to ask the class to remain in their seats during the lesson as there was so much commotion going on. Then in the middle of the lesson, I turned toward the board for just a few seconds to write something. As I turned again to face the class, there directly in front of me was a boy who normally sat at the back. He had gotten out of his seat and quickly walked up to the front of the room to face me as I turned around. He wanted to know what I had written on his report card. I was disappointed with his contempt. He both disobeyed my request to remain in his seat and disrupted the class with something irrelevant to the class as a whole. I simply told him to show the report card to his mother and ask her what it said. Self-control is such an important part of the Fruit of the Holy Spirit and essential in conducting an effective Sunday school class.

In another class, I was forewarned that the third grade teacher had a great deal of trouble with them. I was a relatively new teacher and naively thought that because of the depth of my spirituality and my "learned, attractive" approach, I would have no trouble. How wrong I was! The spirit of contention and apathy toward the program was palpable in the atmosphere from the start. In the course of one of the classes, a boy made an airplane with one of the papers I had handed out. He ostentatiously made motions in preparation for throwing it. I walked over to take it away from him. He refused to give it to me and finally dropped it behind his back. It was retrieved by another boy who proceeded to pick it up and run with it like a football player after recovering a fumble. I finally apprehended the paper airplane. It was a disgraceful and embarrassing scene. When there's a war going on, the entire package of the Fruit of the Spirit is severely tested. A brother offended is harder to win than a city (as given in Proverbs 18:19), and the same is true of a class offended. If the teacher responds in kind to all the mean things the class does, the war goes on, and everyone loses. We need to win the souls and hearts of these children even when they disrupt the class and belittle us. Love and gentleness are our most powerful weapons.

Despite their bravado and misbehavior, little children are helpless and vulnerable. They depend on those who love them. Each child in fourth grade Sunday school deserves to be loved. The Sunday schoolteacher needs to love the little ones God puts in his or her class. This is the work of the Holy Spirit.

If your pastor invites you to teach Sunday school or if you feel led to volunteer, do it. Don't let your feelings of inadequacy or doubts about your spirituality hold you back. It's really God's work and He will see that it gets done. God will give you the help of the Holy Spirit to do the job for which He has selected you.

Chapter 3

Nature of Fourth Grade Sunday Schoolteachers

The soul is healed by being with children.

—**Fyodor Dostoyevsky**

Over 90 percent of the teachers in the Sunday school program at our parish and at many other churches as well are female. Whatever the reason, women have assumed the responsibility for religious education of our young people. It is probably true that women are more spiritual than men by nature. Men, on the other hand, are so consumed by job responsibilities, caring for their families and their homes, involvement in sports, etc., that they have no time for spiritual programs. Perhaps modern macho men can't be concerned with something so unmasculine as fourth grade Sunday school.

This is an unfortunate situation. Children get the impression that religion is not a manly thing and that it's only for women. Yet Jesus was a man among men, strong beyond comprehension in the face of severe opposition and with no human support. At the same time, He was most compassionate and forgiving toward all who came to Him in their need.

Most Sunday schoolteachers are not professionally trained educators. They mimic what their teachers had done. Yet I've seen some very effective instructors in our Sunday school. The love and joy exudes from them as they present these valuable lessons to the children. Laypeople whose hearts are right can be efficient conductors of the light and love of Jesus, as well as sources of wisdom and inspiration to young people.

To give a worldwide perspective on catechesis, one central chapel in a main village in central Zaire serves two hundred surrounding villages. There are no roads connecting these villages. A priest gets around to these villages only twice a year.

In the central chapel, the priest baptizes twenty thousand people at the Easter Vigil Mass in a huge outdoor ceremony, which lasts all day. Catechists are very important to keep the Church going in the villages. Some risk their lives. Recently, when the home office of a missionary society was informed that a catechist in one of the villages had been murdered, the head of the home office volunteered for service in that parish. Amazing how God's work continues in spite of the violence of the world!

One problem with many Sunday schoolteachers is that they usually don't teach very long, some only a year or two before someone else takes over. It's not an easy job, and it takes time and effort. Many are not willing to make the continued sacrifice. Over such a short term, it's not possible to get into a flow, to improve on lesson plans, or to get to know patterns of behavior of the children. Obviously this is not a good thing. The more the continuity and the more persistent the effort from year to year, the better the program. More dedicated teachers would give stability to our religious education programs.

These are troubled times: shootings in schools, high suicide rates among young people, widespread divorce, drug and alcohol abuse, disrespect for the sacredness of sex, materialistic values, etc. Peter Kreeft wrote a book entitled *Back to Virtue*,[4] a very timely and insightful commentary. Kreeft reminds us that the word virtue means "manly strength." Our world has gone astray moving toward false gods and distorted value systems. We need to come back to virtue, and effective Sunday school programs are an important part in the return process. Now is the time for all good men to come to the aid of the Church and society. Where are the men? Surely our churches have about an equal number of males and females. Why is it that essentially only women teach Sunday school? Did Jesus come only for women? Apparently our men are so busy trying to live up to the Clint Eastwood macho concept of manhood that they overlook the authentic manhood of Jesus.

May I mention a strong Christian man who stands out as a model for other men? Bill Gothard has a PhD degree in counseling and is

---

[4] Ignatius Press, Ft. Collins, CO, 1992.

especially concerned about young people with behavioral problems. He explains that there are three root causes of serious problems in human behavior: bitterness, greed, and moral impurity. There are only three root causes but many manifestations of these basic errors. When scriptural principles are violated, all kinds of troubles ensue. Bill tells the story of a teenager in Chicago who had a host of problems: trouble with the law, drug abuse, rebellion toward his parents and other authorities as well as problems in his schoolwork. His parents were deeply concerned and took the boy to a series of psychiatrists. They spent over fifty thousand dollars for psychotherapy but saw no improvement in the boy's life. The psychiatrists analyzed in detail the superficial behavioral abnormalities but never got to the root problem. The parents then brought the boy to Bill Gothard who finally got to the core of the matter. In only a few sessions, Bill uncovered bitterness and unforgiveness toward his father deep within the boy's heart. Once that was made clear to the boy and once he asked for God's grace to help him overcome that bitter root of evil within him, only then did his behavior improve. When we see how God's law has been violated and make amends, only then His graces flow freely to heal our injuries and our lives change.

Where are the men who know the power of Holy Scripture and know the importance of being right with God? Let them come forth and serve the Lord by building strong Sunday school programs and serving as much-needed role models for young children.

Chapter 4

How to Conduct a Fourth Grade Sunday School Class

*As Christians, we know that, for us,
prayer is as essential as breathing.*

—**Pope John Paul II**

There are probably as many ways to conduct a fourth grade Sunday school class as there are teachers. It doesn't matter how, as long as the job gets done—as long as Jesus is lifted up so all the children can know His love.

To teach a good Sunday school class, I believe you must be in the "state of grace" or in other words be right with God and not have any nagging guilt holding you back. Many times, I talk things over with my pastor on Saturday afternoon to get ready for Sunday morning. To effectively do God's work, we should have all channels open to Him and not have anything clogging the pipes. After all, it's His work, and we need to keep the way clear for Him. If our thoughts or actions have not been pure or worthy in God's sight, we need to make amends before facing the class. Then we can be free to love and care for those whom He sends to us. Jesus tells us that fasting and prayer are powerful weapons in spiritual warfare, according to Matthew 17:21. They work for Sunday school too. I routinely fast about eighteen hours prior to teaching a Sunday school class. It clears my head and gives me a deep joy and peace. To me, this is valuable preparation and greatly enhances the effectiveness of my classes.

When I first started teaching in 1985, we had a good fourth grade Sunday school textbook with a simple Bible-based message. It was a joy to prepare a focused lesson from this textbook. After a few years, we decided to purchase new textbooks for all our classes. We didn't use good judgment and started the year with books that were of lesser quality, were loaded with people's opinions, were not focused on a simple theme, and were not written in simple language that the children could read and understand. It was a problem for several weeks, so we went back to our old books. After about two years, our textbooks went out of print, and we were forced to purchase new books. Nevertheless, our Sunday schoolteachers adjusted and presented lessons built on scriptural principles and then illustrated these principles in attractive ways. Frequently, we made copies of lessons from older textbooks to present quality Sunday school classes.

In my case, Saturday night is preparation time for Sunday morning—no socializing, going to a movie, etc. I study and prepare until I have the lesson in mind and go over it several times before I go to bed. For me, a good night's sleep fixes things in mind and makes for a better class.

Also on Saturday night, I invite one of the parents of my Sunday school children to sit in on the class. Mostly, they are glad to do so. Not only do they get to see firsthand what goes on, but also they are valuable as the class is being conducted. They are asked to read inspirational stories to the class. True stories are selected usually from the *Guideposts* magazine, which are generally short, relevant to the lesson, and have deep meaning. This can be a powerful teaching tool. Usually the parents are glad to participate, and they benefit from the stories too. Another advantage of having a parent in the class is I have another adult in the room.

My Sunday school class starts informally. First the children get their Bibles, look up the verse indicated on the board, and write it down on a piece of paper. This appears disorganized but actually is an important part of the class. It gets the students interested in the Holy Scriptures. They learn what the books of the Bible are, what a chapter is, and what a verse is. They complain that the books of the Bible are not in alphabetical order, but they slowly learn the names of the books and something of the nature of many of the books. At first, it's all confusing to them, but by the end of the school year, they are all pretty good at finding verses in the Holy Scriptures. I'm very proud of them when they finally become familiar and comfortable with the Bible and can easily locate any verse they need.

Children really need a good perspective on Holy Scripture, to see the sweetness and strength there and not be intimidated by others who misuse the word of God. When Martin Luther began the Reformation in the year 1517, it caused great arguments based on scripture. These arguments continue to the present day. About ten years before I started teaching Sunday school, I joined my first Bible study group led by a graduate student at Purdue University. I was then fairly ignorant of scripture but was eager to learn and be a part of a dedicated group and come close to God. The motivation of our graduate student leader, however, was to point out that his denomination was the only authentic one, and people in other denominations were going to hell. He quoted one Bible verse after another to "prove" his point. This caused great dissension among the members of this ecumenical gathering. After a few weeks, everyone dropped out of the group. It's hard to describe how hurt and bitterly disappointed I was. Where was all this Christian love and compassion I had been hearing about?

As a reaction to all this kind of contention, the Catholic Church centuries ago suggested that people should not read the Holy Scriptures fearing misinterpretation. This was a big mistake. Why deny people the joy and consolation obtained from reading and contemplating scripture? Few things in life are so beneficial as meditation upon the word of God. President Woodrow Wilson expressed amazement that all people did not devote time to reading the Bible and receiving the profound insight, peace, and direction it provides. Thank God that since Vatican II the Catholic Church has changed and now encourages Bible study by individuals. I believe the fourth grade is a critical time to familiarize children with the wisdom, power, and comfort contained in the Bible.

Although I had little exposure to Holy Scripture in parochial schools, I now feel comfortable with the Bible. I've attended about five thousand prayer meetings and Bible studies and have done much individual study on my own. Also in 1978, I attended Bill Gothard's *Institute in Basic Youth Conflicts* (Box 1, Oak Brook, IL 60521). During the thirty-two lecture hours of the course, thousands of references to Bible verses were given and related to everyday human experiences. I also took a course in the New Testament and one in the Old Testament at Purdue University. Without this background, I would not be as effective as a Sunday schoolteacher.

When the students come into my classroom on Sunday mornings, they immediately get busy writing down their Bible verses. I make it a point to greet them as they come into the room. This simple gesture is important to make them feel welcome and for me to build a personal relationship with each child. Amazingly, about a third of the time, they don't respond to my greeting; they are so distracted.

My classes formally begin with a spontaneous prayer on my part asking a blessing on each child and for God's help with the class and also to acknowledge the parent who is with the class on that particular day. I appreciate their coming and the effort they make to help. Then in about five minutes, I try to encapsulate the purpose of the class. This is reinforced when I ask the students to volunteer to read out loud the paragraphs in their texts. In our books, this is usually a simplified reading from the Bible. A great advantage of teaching fourth grade is that the students can read and write.

When I started teaching Sunday school, the Director of Religious Education (DRE) took me aside and showed me a videotape entitled *Dare to Discipline* by James Dobson. Dr. Dobson was trying to reverse the trend toward social chaos and made these videotapes asking educators and teachers to bring about a revival of effective discipline in the classroom administered in an atmosphere of love and acceptance. The videotape depicted a disorganized scene with the teacher losing control, all kinds of commotion, and unintelligible statements from all around the room. Even the teacher did not make good sense. It was a pathetic picture and made a great impression on me. Even so, I must admit some of my classes resemble the situation depicted by Dobson. A certain control and authority should be maintained by the teacher while reflecting the gentleness of Jesus. With some classes this can be more difficult than others.

After the students read, the central theme of the class is reinforced with a filmstrip. To mention one example, if our textbook has the story of the Prodigal Son, a filmstrip showing the same story is viewed. Having read about it and having seen the filmstrip, the children are asked to reenact the story live. We use stuffed animals (bears and dogs) to represent the characters. It's fun for them and makes a lasting impression.

Then we read true stories from *Guideposts* usually the ones entitled "His Mysterious Ways." They involve amazing things that happen when God intervenes in people's lives. The children may forget some of the lessons, but when I happen to meet students years after they have left my class, they tell me they still recall the stories. When examples of how God directly intervenes in everyday circumstances are shared, it builds everybody's faith.

The singing we do in our worship services is an important way to honor God and brings joy and peace to the hearts of those who join their voices together to glorify their Creator. In our local parish prayer group, we spend about 45 percent of our weekly meeting time just singing and acknowledging God's greatness, mercy, and goodness in songs. It brings a great freedom and deep-down sense of well-being and gratitude for all we have been given by Him. Why not praise God with singing in Sunday school also? The idea that you should take time out in the class just to enjoy yourself singing songs to honor God is a good one. The purpose of the class is not only to learn something about God, but also to experience the joy that He alone can give. Accordingly, talented musicians from local parishes have been invited to sing and play guitar for our students. Although it's difficult to arrange for these sessions, some of the children seem to appreciate it. It's kind of a spectacle to them, but for the most part they enjoy it. Also, I've tried without accompaniment to have the children join me in simple songs of praise. However, doing it formally in the middle of class doesn't seem to work. Many don't sing along and just sit there and glare at me and don't seem to like it at all. But if I sing simple songs like "This Little Light of Mine" during the time they are writing their Bible verses, some will sing along and others just continue to write their verses but don't mind the singing. It seems to work well that way.

Our parish has two serial filmstrips each with ten episodes, which tell simple stories about experiences children have and which mention Bible verses pertinent to the stories. They are well done and are entertaining as well as instructive. These are shown toward the end of the class. They maintain the students' attention and send them home relaxed.

We have a rule that the children should not bring drinks into class. In our experience when they do bring drinks, invariably there's a spill and the floor gets sticky, also no donuts with all that gooey icing. We do provide animal crackers for the children to eat during the filmstrips. We seem to have cookie monsters in each class.

Often a few minutes remain at the end of class. We use this time for "prayers of the faithful." Jesus told us to ask for what we need, according to John 16:24. So I invite the kids to pray at that time. We get varied responses about healing for a grandmother with cancer or for a blue tetra (a fish) that's not doing well or for a soccer game coming up. This too is an important part of the class, which reminds the children that we have a God who cares for us and wants to help us in both simple and important matters, according to Matthew 10:30.

Purdue athletes seen in the back row visiting our Sunday school class. My high school helper is on the left in the second row.

One of our Sunday school classrooms with metal chairs. Note the nature scenes on the wall.

Twenty-five Years in the Fourth Grade 29

Students writing their Bible verses. Visiting parents use chairs in back of room.

Blessed Sacrament Church in winter. Janine Reklaitis is a long time member of Blessed Sacrament and one of the pillars of our Church. She wrote the preface to this book.

Chapter 5

True Stories of How God Works in People's Lives

*I have lived a long time, Sir, and the longer I live,
the more convincing proof I see of this truth,
that God governs in the affairs of men.*

—Ben Franklin

To be a good Christian, we need to love God whom we cannot see, cannot hear, and cannot touch. Most people find it easy to love their families. They can see, hear, and touch them and directly share sorrows and joys with them. But to love this mysterious "far off" God doesn't come so naturally or so easily. It's difficult for adults as well as children. Yet Jesus told us that not only should we love God, but we should also do so with all our heart, all our mind, all our soul, and all our strength, as given in Mark 12:30. This is asking a lot from each one of us, especially from fourth grade children.

An important integral part of my Sunday school classes involves sharing true stories of how God intervenes in the lives of ordinary people. God performed miracles in Biblical times, and He still does so in this day and age. I mentioned previously the stories we read in each class from *Guideposts* magazine. These are incredible things that happen and in many cases are beyond human comprehension. Yet they occur and can be appreciated by fourth graders.

Stories of how God reveals Himself help us to know and appreciate our loving heavenly Father. Miracles have occurred throughout history. Healings by Jesus and all the wonders recorded in the Book of Acts and in the Old Testament assure us that God loves us; they help us love Him too. Miracles continue to the present time.

Through the years the "chicken story" has been a favorite in my classes. A waitress in Milwaukee got off work late one night. The special that day was fried chicken, and the manager told her to take some of the leftovers with her. She wrapped them in plastic and put them in a bag and left. Because she got off late, she missed the last bus home and didn't have money for a taxi. She prayed to God to get her home safely. As she walked through the deserted streets of downtown Milwaukee, she passed an alley where a man with a knife jumped out, grabbed her, and told her he was taking her to his place. With the knife pointed at her back, she was terrified and didn't dare scream. She began to cry and her knees were shaking. "Why have you abandoned me, O God? I asked you to get me home safely," she cried.

Just then she heard a voice say, "Debbie, eat your chicken." Obviously, she didn't feel like eating chicken at a time like that. She complained again that God had let her down. Then she heard the voice, once more, saying, "Debbie, eat your chicken." So she took the chicken out of the bag and out of the plastic and held it in her hands, still not wanting to eat it. When they passed two dogs rummaging in the garbage, the dogs smelled the chicken and growling came over to the lady. The man with the knife ran off. The lady tore off pieces of chicken and threw them to the dogs who fought over them. She continued to tear off chicken pieces for the dogs who followed her all the way home. It seemed like God had abandoned her, yet she got home safely. How often in our own lives do we feel God has let us down, and yet when we keep trying to do the right thing it all seems to work out. The children appreciate the humor in the story and the assurance that God does hear our prayers.

A precious *Guideposts* story we read at Christmas time involves a man and his wife who owned an appliance store somewhere in the southeast. It was a small town store that sold almost anything, and at Christmas nearly all their stock of toys was sold out. They were tired after they closed the store on Christmas Eve and looked forward to attending the church service that night and having a relaxing holiday. They had one son who was a teenager, so the excitement of having a small child was missing that year. They woke up that morning and had a quiet Christmas with the tree and all the trimmings and a nice breakfast. The son went off to visit a friend, the father went back to bed, and the wife did the dishes. While cleaning up, she felt a need to go to the store.

That's silly, she thought, *there will be no one there on Christmas morning.* Besides the weather was bad with ice and snow, and a cold wind was blowing. Yet she couldn't shake the urge to go down to the store. She told her husband that she was going, and he asked, "What on earth for?" She said she felt she just had to go, and he replied, "OK, but be careful." Dressed warmly with overshoes, she started her walk to the store. The sleet stung her cheeks as she slowly made her way along the empty streets. As she neared the store, she noticed two little boys looking into the store window. One of them saw her and said, "Here she comes. See I told you she would come." The smaller of the two boys had been crying. The lady opened the store and turned up the heat. The boys warmed their hands by the stove. The elder boy explained that Jimmie didn't get anything for Christmas, and he wanted a pair of skates. The lady said they were nearly out of toys except for a layaway package which no one had picked up. She unwrapped the package, and miraculously it contained a pair of roller skates. Even more surprising, the skates fit Jimmie perfectly. The boys tried to give the lady three dollars, but she told them to buy gloves for themselves. Their eyes widened when they realized she was giving them the skates. As they were leaving the store, the lady asked how they knew she would be at the store on Christmas morning. They said they knew she would be there because they prayed that Jesus would send her. The lady went home, and when her son returned and some relatives had come for Christmas dinner, they had the most joyous Christmas ever. Although not always rational, God prompts us toward the most appropriate, heartwarming experiences. Thank you, God, for guiding us in your ways of peace, helpfulness, and generosity.

    Another favorite of mine is the story of a young man from North Carolina who had an argument with his mother and left home. He wandered across the United States working at various jobs including working as a hospital orderly, gas station attendant, and a plumber's assistant. Then after about two years, he decided that he had wandered around enough and headed for home. He had little money so he hitchhiked. He got as far as High Point, NC, and then had trouble getting a ride. He was tired and hungry. He heard someone call his name from across the road. It was his stepfather. He asked his stepfather how he happened to be there at that time. He answered that the boy's mother had told him to come. She had been reading her Bible and knew that her son was coming home and would be at that place, which was not too far from their home. The son did not write or call, but still the mother knew he would be at that location at that specific time. How did she know? There is a God who arranges things and communicates important information to those who are attuned to Him.

A story about a dream that wouldn't go away involves a rancher in the Utah-Wyoming area of the Rocky Mountains. A small plane had crashed in the mountains in November. Four hundred planes were sent out to search for the lost aircraft, but, failing to find it after four days of searching, they gave up. The rancher went to bed that night and prayed that the plane would be found and that the passengers, a young doctor and his wife, would be safe. During the night he had a dream that he was flying a small plane over the mountains and that he had spotted the downed plane. He clearly saw a red fuselage sticking out of the white snow and people were standing by the plane. (The color of the plane was never mentioned on the newscasts.) He woke from the dream but didn't think much of it since he had prayed for those people before going to sleep. He then went back to sleep and had the same dream again. This time when he woke up, he got out a map of the area (he had hunted and fished in the mountains when he was younger) and thought he knew just about where the downed plane was. Going back to sleep, he had the same dream a third time, this time from a farther distance so he was pretty sure where those people were. Waking in the morning, he turned on the radio and learned that the search for the downed plane had definitely been called off and that there was not much chance of finding those people alive since the temperature had gone down below zero each night since the crash. Even if they survived the accident, they probably would have frozen to death.

The rancher had chores to do, the cattle needed to be fed, but after he finished, he felt he had to do something about his dream. He was a student pilot, so he went down to the local country airport. The manager was gone, and although he did not have a pilot's license, he got the teenage boy who was minding the airport to help him roll one of the planes out of the hangar. He took off and soon was over the area he had seen in his dream. At first, he couldn't find the downed plane and became frightened, but then he saw the red fuselage sticking out of the snow and the people waving just as in the dream. He returned to the airport and was verbally abused by the airport manager for flying the plane without permission, but he finally convinced him that he had found the lost plane. He called the Civil Air Patrol and arranged for supplies to be dropped to the doctor and his wife by plane. A ground rescue party was organized, and it took twenty-four hours for the horses to reach the site through six-foot snowdrifts. The couple had only a candy bar to eat for four days and huddled together in the cockpit of the downed plane to keep from freezing. They did not sleep for four days but prayed earnestly for God to send help. They didn't dream God could be so specific in answering those prayers.

Sometimes I share with my classes a personal example of how the Holy Spirit can change the life of a young person. My son, Jon, played baseball in high school. He was always well coordinated but not very big. He started some games at first base as a junior and was outstanding defensively but did not hit all that well. I remember late in that season they were playing an important conference away game and were behind by a couple of runs in the last inning. They put Jon in as a pinch hitter with men on base. I just knew he wasn't well prepared and wouldn't get a hit. Sure enough he struck out. That next fall, we attended a Full Gospel Businessman's meeting. The main speaker was a fine Christian man who was a bodybuilder. He gave a fascinating talk and demonstrated his strength by bending thick metal spikes with his bare hands. He told the fathers not to send their sons out to compete athletically without being prepared. He suggested a program to increase the body strength. I didn't say anything to Jon, but he took it on himself to build up his strength in preparation for his senior year. For example, he would stand on his hands, put his toes on the wall of his room, and do twenty whole body pushups. Come spring he was very strong and in great shape. He batted .428 that season, and his team won the conference co-championship. If Jon had had another mediocre season, it would have affected his whole life. He learned that with prayer and proper training he could be outstanding against stiff competition. Jon now has three children of his own and has a supervisory position as a civil engineer. Amazing how God works in people's lives!

My other son Peter also played high school baseball. I pray a lot for him too. He got eight straight base hits when put in the games as a pinch hitter; this was a minor miracle. Because Christ rose from the dead, we know miracles happen and that the Lord answers our prayers. Lastly my daughter, Lynn Anne, was baptized by Father Zahn at Blessed Sacrament in March 1980 when she was about three months old. She was crying, fussing, and acting up; I thought we would have to cancel the whole thing. But when the water was poured over her head, she immediately became quiet. The calming effect of the Holy Spirit is powerful and available to each one of us, young and old.

Chapter 6

Characteristics of Students in Fourth Grade Sunday School

You cannot be what you are not but you can become what you are not.

—One-Minute Pocket Bible for the business professional, 1994

    Fourth grade Sunday school students are not as serious about Sunday school as they are about regular school. Their homework from public school takes precedence over anything the Sunday schoolteacher may assign. One little girl informed me that she didn't have time to memorize the Twenty-third Psalm because she had to do her homework. Many children and adults don't realize God is our number one priority. Scripture study should be an obligation of every one of us who desires to enter into that fullness of life promised by Jesus, as given in John 10:10.

    An interesting characteristic of fourth graders is that they are masters of the non sequitur. Psychologists have found that many twelve-year-olds are willing to stop the class to mention something remotely related to what is being discussed. Once we were reading about a man who was severely burned over 80 percent of his body and was not expected to live. When the skin is extensively injured, body fluids are lost, red blood cells are destroyed, and these patients are hypersusceptible to infection. God brought about a miracle in this man's life, and he was healed. We were trying to show how compassionate God is and how He helped this man in time of great need. One little boy raised his hand and mentioned that his aunt is a nurse, and she has a friend who was in a hotel when it caught on fire. Luckily, the friend wasn't injured. Another time when discussing Joan of Arc, we mentioned that army generals were usually old men with beards, not teenage girls. One young lady raised her hand and mentioned that women in ancient Egypt used to wear false beards to make themselves look like men. One great challenge of the fourth grade Sunday schoolteacher is to respond to disparate comments and then recapture the flow of the lesson even when repeated distractions occur.

Catechists should be aware of Abraham Maslow's (1908-1970) "Hierarchy of Needs" discussed by Ristow.[5] Only when basic needs are satisfied are students able to learn properly. When hunger and thirst are satisfied, then students can move up to the second level to satisfy the need for safety and security. Feeling safe and secure, children enter the third level, seeking acceptance and love. When acceptance and love prevail, children can achieve competency, approval, and recognition. Thus our job as catechists is to provide for all these basic needs (some come to Sunday school with no breakfast) so that each child will be able to perform well and fully comprehend the lessons presented. Ristow also indicates that the attention span is proportional to the age so that a first grader (six years old) can pay attention for about six minutes and a seventh grader (thirteen years old) can do so for thirteen to fifteen minutes.

In any randomly selected group of fourth graders we have a spectrum of spiritual orientation. Some are from God-centered families who pray together and show great reverence for God. Others are from families which are not God oriented. A good Sunday schoolteacher aims to meet the needs of each student in the class. The lessons should be simple and clear so that children from any spiritual background can benefit from them.

Father Dan Davis O. P., former Pastor of St. Thomas Aquinas Parish in West Lafayette, IN, said, "Sunday school draws the child into the faith community." Mass doesn't do it. They don't understand the significance of the ritual. No wonder they always seem to be crawling under the

---

[5] Kate Ristow, *Catechist Magazine,* September 2001, p. 26-29.

pews. Effective Sunday school instruction is a lifesaver for our children and makes the risen Christ real to them.

Families have a great influence, but individuals have to make their own decision to accept Christ. As they say, God has no grandchildren. I'm reminded of a student in one of my classes who was from a very God-centered family. His father was one of our best Sunday schoolteachers. This boy was sharp and quickly caught on to finding verses in the Bible, so much so that he would direct other students to the proper pages. This upset me because I think the students learn by fumbling through the Bible in search of different books, chapters, and verses. As the school year wore on, it became clear that this student wasn't really very serious about his faith, even for a ten-year-old. When asked what he was giving up for Lent, he maintained he wasn't giving up anything. The practice of little acts of self-denial during Lent is important spiritually. One wise man once said that it is in self-denial, not in self-indulgence, that we find peace and joy. Giving up candy, soda pop, or ice cream during Lent is a small act of reverence for God indicating He alone is sufficient for us. Yet this student refused to enter into the spirit of this most holy penitential season. It amazes me that some students from God-oriented families can go through the motions, seemingly pay attention to the Sunday school lessons, and yet not really want to be a part of the Kingdom or really be supportive of the whole Sunday school effort.

Some students are quiet and peaceful, are attentive to the lessons, and make supportive, insightful comments. Any teacher is glad to have such students. Thank God I've had a few in each of my classes. They make the whole effort so much more worthwhile. They balance out those students who just can't sit still and would rather be outside. In some cases, we are called just to plant seeds, knowing that someone else will see the results.

Mostly, students in fourth grade Sunday school are just like people in general. They need to be appreciated. They need positive reinforcement. If they successfully locate a Bible verse or complete a Bible-based crossword puzzle, they need to be praised. They also want to make an important contribution to the class. I've heard some profound theological statements from ten-year-olds. Once I commented on Jesus's washing the apostles' feet, saying it was an amazing act of humility for the Creator of the universe. One little girl mentioned that maybe it was just what He was supposed to do—to care for those He loves. And right she was; each time He reaches down to purify and support his soiled, frightened, and lost sheep, He shows us His compassionate, loving nature. A well-conducted and inspired fourth grade Sunday school lesson provides strokes and learning for students, for any parents who attend, and for the teacher also.

On another occasion, I mentioned the story behind the Jewish Passover, when the Jews sacrificed the Paschal Lamb and marked the doorposts of their houses with the lamb's blood so that the Lord would not enter but would "pass over" all Jewish households. However, each of the other households in Egypt woke up to find their eldest child dead. How awful those families must have felt that morning at the loss of their eldest children! One of the little girls in the class raised her hand and asked, "What happened to forgiveness and mercy?" She said those eldest children of Egyptian families were not responsible for the pharaoh's actions. I had to agree with her and said I really don't understand God completely myself. Little children can have profound theological insight.

C. S. Lewis once said, "Joy is the serious business of heaven." Therefore, laughter is very appropriate during a Sunday school class. Ten—to eleven-year-old children are beginning to develop a sense of humor. So we tell silly jokes like, "When a dog quarterback throws a pass, to whom does he throw it?"

Answer, "A Labrador receiver." Or, "What did Scooby Doo say while eating a hotdog?" Answer, "It's a dog-eat-dog world." The kids tell some of their own. One boy asked, "What's green and pecks on a tree?" "Woody Wood pickle." It took me a while to get that one, but I really appreciated the dry sense of humor there. One Sunday, a little boy mentioned that he was considering going into the priesthood. I told him I was overjoyed and happy for him. The very next week, he was flirting with one of the little girls in the class. I said to him, "I thought you were going to be a priest?" He hesitated and then answered, "Well, I'm going to enjoy my childhood first." I got such a kick out of what he said that I called his parents and shared it with them. Children in the fourth grade are not able to understand just any joke, and sometimes will tell what they think is a joke, but it's not funny at all. This calls for restraint and ingenuity on the part of the teacher to respond in a clever way without hurting anyone's feelings.

Chapter 7

Role of the Holy Spirit in Fourth Grade Sunday School

Adventure is the champagne of life.

—**G. K. Chesterton**

A satisfying experience in teaching fourth grade Sunday school is to have everything in the lesson fall into place, even the unplanned things. I usually don't have a chance to preview all parts of the filmstrips that will be shown, but often scenes depicted fit in very well. In a class on the Seventh Commandment, "Thou shalt not steal," one of the filmstrips showed a neighborhood bully trying to steal a little boy's bike. Fortunately, the mother appears just in time. Another class on the Fifth commandment, "Thou shalt not kill," a filmstrip included a part on Albert Schweitzer and his concept of reverence for life. I'm so grateful to God for His input and help in preparation and presentation of these important lessons which illustrate principles for successful living.

Jesus told us (as given in John 16:13) that the Holy Spirit would guide us into all truth. I believe it's essential to invite the Holy Spirit to inspire, direct, and lead the Sunday school class. That Christianity has survived for two thousand years and is strong and flourishing is evidence that God's Holy Spirit is active and powerful. The Holy Spirit supports all our efforts to serve the Lord and is especially active in Sunday school.

Essentially, the Sunday schoolteacher deals with people. Knowing the four basic personality types provides wisdom and insight in understanding the parents who sit in on the class each week, other adults in the program as well as yourself. Children in the fourth grade do not have fully developed personalities and really don't have much chance to express themselves so it's difficult to classify them according to the personality type.[6] Examples of the basic personality types are as follows: the apostle, Peter, the "sanguine," talkative, outgoing, and compassionate but also weak-willed, undependable, and fearful type; Paul, the "choleric," domineering crafty, and cruel but also determined, productive, and decisive type; Moses, the "melancholy," moody, rigid, and impractical but also sensitive, idealistic, and humble type; lastly, Abraham, "phlegmatic," diplomatic, calm, and conservative but sometimes selfish, indecisive, and unmotivated type. We can categorize everyone we meet accordingly, realizing that most people are mixtures of these four basic types. The idea is not to condemn or judge or avoid people but to encourage and work with their strengths while also bearing in mind that each of these temperaments can be very lovable under the influence of the Holy Spirit. Saul, before his conversion, was despicable and probably had few friends, but afterward Paul was greatly loved, and people hugged him and kissed him on the neck and cried at the thought of not seeing him again, according to Acts 29:37-38.

In my case, I would not even be in the Sunday school program had it not been for the Holy Spirit. I was baptized in the Holy Spirit at a Full Gospel businessmen's Fellowship International (FGBFI) meeting in October 1978. Even though I had received the sacrament of confirmation in the Catholic Church, this Full Gospel event was a pivotal experience in my life. Saint Paul asked the Ephesians (Acts 19:2), "Did you receive the Holy Spirit?" They answered that they had not so much as heard of the Holy Spirit. I too was ignorant of what the Holy Spirit could do in my life. Not that I wasn't told about it or that the sacrament of confirmation is of no value, but I had to make a public admission of my great need for the Spirit of God in my life at the age of forty-two. When I came to Purdue University to teach pharmacology in the Pharmacy School in 1969, I was not even attending church regularly. Who would have guessed that I would be able to teach fourth grade Sunday school for twenty-five consecutive years? The Holy Spirit not only helps us to conduct our Sunday school classes, but also calls us to become involved in the first place.

---

[6] Tim LaHaye, *Transformed Temperaments*, Tyndale House Publishers, Wheaton, IL, 1982.

Chapter 8

The Role of God-Oriented Wisdom in Teaching Sunday School

I found more wisdom in prayer at the feet of the Crucified than in all the books I ever read.

—St. Thomas Aquinas

Some believe that wisdom is a gift of God and cannot be obtained by our own efforts, apart from God. Holy Scripture supports this belief since James 1:5 says, "If any of you lacks wisdom, let him ask of God who gives to all liberally and without reproach and it will be given to him." Wisdom and godly insight are needed in every aspect of our lives, in our families, in our communities, in our jobs, and in our government. I believe a special point should be made to each Sunday school class to remind them that they all need wisdom to function well in this complex society, and wisdom comes only from God.

Several chapters from Proverbs pertain to wisdom. In chapter 1:2, it says Proverbs was written that we may know wisdom and perceive words of understanding. "Wisdom is better than rubies and all things that one desires cannot be compared with her" (Prov. 8:11). In chapter 9, verse 10, it says, "The fear of the Lord is the beginning of wisdom." In other words, we first have to get to know God and to deeply respect Him and fully appreciate His ways before we can have wisdom. We don't just go to school and accumulate various degrees to become wise. A man with a PhD degree by the name of Earl Sutherland received the Nobel

Prize for his discovery of the mechanism by which glucose is mobilized from the liver by epinephrine and glucagon. This was a truly amazing discovery that Dr. Sutherland made in his forties. Yet he seemed to lack practical, godly wisdom since he was an alcoholic and died at the age of fifty-nine. This great gift does not come easily. Only by being open to God and aware of His presence do we come to "fear," i.e., respect the Lord and have the beginning of wisdom.

I remember my mother encouraging me when I was a teenager to pray that God would grant me wisdom. I did so but did not open my heart to receive the gift and did not have the proper respect for (fear of) Him. I first had to experience more of the cold, merciless ways of the world before I could earnestly seek to know Him and to appreciate God's ways.

Wisdom is not intelligence. There are many intelligent people who have little spiritual wisdom. According to Webster's dictionary, intelligence is mental acuteness or shrewdness. The wisdom (intelligence) of the world is folly with God, according to 1 Corinthians 3:19. Remember the shrewd steward of the rich man who wasted his masters' goods, as given in Luke 16. When he was asked to give an accounting, he called in his masters' debtors and decreased the amounts owed. The master commended the dishonest steward for his shrewdness and said that the sons of this world are shrewder in dealing with the world than are the Sons of Light. His master told him that he could no longer be a steward. This steward obviously was an intelligent man but not wise in godly ways.

I believe godly wisdom includes prudence, good judgment, and appropriate behavior. The Bible says, "I wisdom dwell in prudence and find out knowledge and discretion" (Prov. 8:12). Wisdom involves discernment and good common sense. The other gifts of the Holy Spirit (understanding, fortitude, counsel, knowledge, piety, and fear of the Lord) are also important for effective Sunday school instruction, but I believe wisdom with appropriate conduct is the most important of all.

I must share with you a true story about a general in World War II in Europe. The advance of his army was being held up by some German soldiers barricaded in a farmhouse. The general went to that area and asked the captain in charge what the problem was. The captain said, "Sir, they're shooting at us."

The general said, "Let me show you how to attack a farmhouse." He gathered the men around him, and they threw several grenades at the farmhouse and then as a unit ran toward the house firing their weapons and yelling. The Germans exited by the rear door. The general then said to the captain, "That's how you attack a farmhouse." Satan is always going to be shooting at us, but we need to go ahead anyway and attack the farmhouse.

Chapter 9

Each Class Has a Different Personality

You have made us for yourself, O Lord, and our hearts are restless until they rest in You.

—St. Augustine of Hippo

It's well known by teachers that classes have different characteristics, just like individuals. Somewhat different approaches need to be taken depending on the nature of the class. What works in one class may not work in another.

The most pleasant class I ever had was a very quiet, respectful one. They allowed the lessons to be presented without interruption or distraction, and the whole year was a pure joy. Any questions asked were pertinent and insightful. Most of the students in the class were open to what was being taught. At the end of the year, I felt good about what we had accomplished even though I knew there were a couple of students in the class I hadn't reached. Despite that, the class as a whole seemed to have found that peace that the world cannot give. They seemed to be able to block out the noisy world we live in and enter into a supernatural peace. It was a very profound thing to witness. Amazingly, one of the teachers who later had this same class complained that they were too quiet. That teacher felt the need to play the radio during class to offset the quietness!

By contrast, the most frustrating class I ever had was noisy and caustic and seemed bent on not allowing the class to be presented. There were all kinds of distractions: ill-timed, irrelevant questions and comments, rattling of chairs, excessive interaction between students, silly statements, etc. The miracle was that I presented the lessons as best I could, trying to maintain the flow of the discussion despite everything. At the end of the year, I was drained and completely discouraged. Even so, I had the feeling that the Holy Spirit did His work, and lives were changed and enhanced in that class. Just because I didn't look good or perform well in the class doesn't mean that the Holy Spirit did not do His job.

In one class, we had a few ten-year-old "professors" who would stop the class to try to enter into philosophical discussions. I appreciated their inquisitiveness but hesitated to take class time to answer "off-the-cuff" questions not pertinent to the class. My answers to questions like "Are there ghosts?" or "Do angels really exist?" or "Have you ever seen a ghost?" were brief and I hope respectful.

Another class had a few ten-year-old "generals." They knew just how the class should be conducted and would point out things to be done. "It's time for a break," or "Don't we get animal crackers to eat during the filmstrip?" or "Don't we get our report cards today?" One boy made a suggestion that we read a story in our books that we had skipped. When we read it, he reminded us that he was the one who suggested we do it. Admittedly, I sometimes overlook things, but ten-year-old generals can be difficult to live with.

I think TV is an insidious evil influence on the characters of our Sunday school students although there are a few good programs available. I don't have a TV, and I don't want one. I believe it has a detrimental effect on adults as well as ten—to eleven-year-olds, gives them false values, decreases the attention span, makes them insensitive to other people, teaches them violence, and gives them distorted self-images (sometimes positive, sometimes negative). With TV, you allow all kinds of characters to come into your home, some of whom represent the worst kinds of evil in the world. Is it worth it to jeopardize your family's integrity to see the few good programs available? The commercials alone are enough to scramble your brain flitting from one scene to another accompanied by loud noises. I've noticed that seminar speakers at Purdue who give good, coherent, logical seminars are generally people who don't watch TV. A good fourth grade Sunday schoolteacher needs to work to overcome the disruptive influence of TV on the lives of young people.

Chapter 10

Factors Affecting Our Sunday School Classes

*Death changes nothing. If we don't learn to praise,
thank and enjoy God now, we never will.*

**—Dorothy Day, Cofounder of the
Catholic Worker Movement**

Certainly the presence of the Spirit of the risen Christ is the most important factor influencing our Sunday school classes. Before each class, I pray that the risen Christ be with us and guide each one of us. The objective is to lift Him higher so that everyone will be drawn unto Him. We should all focus on Jesus in each class and earnestly try to forget ourselves and learn to love Him more. I am seventy-seven years old this year, and from that perspective I can say the greatest thing in life is love, especially that deep, intimate love of our Creator. The purpose of the CCD program is to bring everyone involved closer to the God who loves us beyond imagination.

Although the inspiration to teach Sunday school is a private calling, the teacher needs family support. I'm single now, but I have had my sons, Jon and Peter, each come and speak to my Sunday school classes. They did a fine job. I'm very proud to say that I can talk to them about spiritual things, and they fully understand. When they were young, they accompanied me to the Full Gospel Businessmen's Meetings and also to the Bill Gothard Seminars in "Basic Youth conflicts." They have been supportive of my efforts in the Sunday school program. For married Sunday schoolteachers, the spouse as well as the rest of the family bears some of the burden and should be consulted before accepting the responsibility. I'm deeply indebted to Joann Clark, my good friend, for her love and prayerful support and for her godly influence in my life.

In the wake of the attacks of September 11, 2001, and also now during the Iraq war, it's obvious to me that our political situation filters down into the Sunday school classroom. For example, on the weekend after 9/11, one little boy fell sound asleep in the middle of my class. This had never happened before and has not happened since. He didn't even wake up during the film or when the other students went on break. I made no attempt to wake him and simply went on with the class. Not until the class was over, nearly an hour after he dozed off, did he finally arouse himself and sleepily make his way out of the classroom. So intense was the emotion of our whole nation at that time that this young man felt extremely uptight until he came into the presence of the Living Christ there in Sunday school and finally relaxed to the point of falling asleep. Children now seem to be a little more serious, and CCD attendance is better with our nation at war and with the economy so bad. God has His ways of drawing people to Him.

The "War on Terrorism" and the economic climate make us all paranoid and insecure, giving us more reasons to turn to God for peace and consolation. But with all the legal objections to public prayer or any other references to God in our society, along with legal abortion and same sex marriage, some of our children may be more doubtful and less open to spiritual training. Just as Abraham bargained with God that He not destroy Sodom since there were a few righteous people there, we and our children should be among those faithful few, strengthened by the Holy Spirit to resist evil and be confident in the mercy of God, as given in Genesis 18:23.

Having a helper in the class is invaluable. I've had the help of high school students in several of my classes over the years, and it's a great blessing to have someone who supports your efforts in an intelligent, God-oriented way and who has good judgment in helping to handle the class. They take attendance, help pass out animal crackers, answer questions, sharpen pencils, and generally make the class go more smoothly. The Sunday school lessons are important, and the less time consumed by administrative and practical details, the better. An added benefit is that the helpers see how you conduct a Sunday school class and can learn to do it themselves. It's a healthy thing for the whole program.

Chapter 11

Chain of Command

Stubbornness we deprecate,
Firmness we condone,
The former is our neighbors trait,
The latter is our own.

—John Wooden ("They Call Me Coach."
McGraw-Hill, 1988)

The bishop is ultimately responsible for the Sunday school programs in his diocese. There is a CCD office at the diocesan level, and the director reports to the bishop. The diocese periodically sends out people to speak to the CCD teachers of individual parishes. The diocesan officials are responsible for certifying Sunday schoolteachers based on experience and training. They try to fairly evaluate each teacher based on courses taken, meetings attended, etc. There is an intangible quality, however, that's hard to evaluate, so a teacher with practically no certification can be a very good teacher and a fully certified teacher may not be very effective. I believe the extent to which the teacher is open to the leading of the Holy Spirit is the crucial factor and determines the degree of success. It's love that makes the world go round as they say, and it's love that goes into making a good Sunday school program.

In individual parishes, the pastor is responsible for Sunday school programs, and he delegates that responsibility to the Director of Religious Education (DRE). Since the pastor in most parishes is an extremely busy man, the DRE essentially handles the administrative details. Even though the pastor makes policies, the everyday administrative duties and problems are handled by the DRE. The pastor just wants things to go well and would prefer not to handle problems.

So the DRE is a very important person in the parish. In my twenty-five years in the fourth grade, I have had five DREs, all female, and they have all been very good. They have also been very different in their approaches.

One of my DREs was a go-getter, very outgoing, and discipline oriented. She demanded that we have lesson plans submitted to her for each class. Once toward the end of the school year, I asked if we really needed a lesson plan for that week since we were going to change books at the end of the year. She would not let me off the hook even though that lesson plan would be used only once. She also encouraged the teachers to employ discipline in the classroom. That is very difficult for me since I have a hard time doing both teaching and disciplining at the same time. So I usually just try to have a good class and maintain the student's attention to minimize discipline problems. She once chided me for missing some opportunities to discipline. The DRE was a little dogmatic in her organizational approach. In her CCD teachers' meetings, she would ask each teacher to describe one event that occurred in one of their classes. We were to go around the table in doing so. This is not an easy format for some people, me included. I sometimes get very nervous and uptight at such a procedure so that it's difficult for me to come up with an interesting and significant incident and clearly communicate the situation. The group would get tense and giggle at anything. On one occasion, there was so much tension that one of the teachers broke down and cried while trying to relate her story. However, this DRE was a good person, and I learned a lot from her.

A conflict arose, and a great argument occurred when one of the teachers referred to the creation story in the Bible as a myth. The DRE defended the Bible and insisted that we accept what is written there. Of course, since no human was present at the creation of the universe, the creation story is a myth.[7] Calling the creation story a myth doesn't mean it's in error. It is an explanation of the origin of the universe and mankind. The essence of the story is that God is the Creator. The details of how it was done are not established scientifically by what is in the Bible. A

---

[7] William O'Malley, *Scripture and Myth*, Paulist Press, New York, NY, 1980.

day in Genesis may be a billion years. God could have accomplished the job in any way He wanted. After all, He is God. He could even have done it by evolution. To me the argument over creation is immaterial. The important fact is that God created us and everything else. How He did it may be interesting to debate, but it really doesn't alter the fact that we exist. Some people insist that God created in a certain way and according to a certain schedule. God has no limits and could have created in any of many imaginative ways. In any case, several teachers quit after this confrontation.

Another DRE was more laid back and also had a pleasing, outgoing personality. She was sensitive to others' feelings and conducted informative teacher's meetings. She instructed us in ways of entertaining as well as teaching. One point she made was that we need to keep teaching and not let distractions control us. We also had an interesting series of discussions on the letters of St. Paul. This DRE had the advantage of having taught third grade Sunday school for several years, and she was good at it. She loved the students and knew how to handle them. Some teachers constantly yell at the children to tell them what to do but the children pay no attention, but this DRE was an effective teacher and the children listened to her. She was effective as a DRE also.

During this DRE's tenure, we remodeled our church and had to use classrooms in a local public school to conduct our Sunday school program. (The rooms were available on weekends.) Never did I have it so good. I had ample space, a large blackboard, large windows, good seating for students (round tables big enough for five people), and we even had a sink. What a contrast to our metal student desks with narrow tops from which books constantly fall off. It's important to have adequate facilities and to make what you have attractive for the students. One classroom I had was a former basement storage room with a low ceiling. It was not the best, but I decorated the walls and bulletin board with nature scenes from old calendars so there was a pleasant atmosphere.

The Sunday schoolteacher needs to report on student progress and needs to interact with those in authority, especially when problems arise. However, I've found that it's best to solve your own problems (through prayer and fasting) rather than make them a big issue with administration. Knowing that any or all children will misbehave at times, the best way to deal with problems is to forgive and simply love them. One mechanism we have in dealing with serious behavior problems is the pink slip. This is a statement sent in the mail to the parent of the student involved explaining what happened, and the student and the parent are required to appear at the next class as the student presents a statement as to why they come to Sunday school. I did this for the paper airplane incident mentioned before. The boy involved was from a broken home. The mother came to class with her son, and the boy read a nicely prepared statement explaining his motivation for attending CCD. Overall, however, the pink slip didn't change anything. The boy still was not open to the lessons and had closed his heart to the love and joy that the program should provide. The mother was not happy about the whole incident either. Furthermore, the DRE began to have doubts about my abilities as a teacher and rightfully so. Thus, no one gains from these confrontations. Seeking ways of peace and unity using God's grace and the power of the Holy Spirit is the best approach.

I've learned that I need to be careful what I say about each student on their report cards. I try to be as positive as I can about each student. Also, if I'm having trouble with a class, I need to be discreet in discussing the problems because these statements become exaggerated.

As it says in Ephesians 6:11-18, "We war not against flesh and blood but against principalities, against powers, against rulers of darkness in this age and against spiritual hosts of wickedness in heavenly places." Many people may think this is so much pious babble, but I believe scripture is true and that Satan would be most pleased to disrupt a Sunday school program. Each person involved, the pastor, the DRE, and all the teachers, should prepare themselves to "take on the whole armor of God that you may be able to stand in an evil day and having done all stand."

"Above all taking the shield of faith with which you will be able to quench all of the fiery darts of the wicked one. Praying always with all prayer and supplication in the Spirit, being watchful to this end with all perseverance and supplication for all the saints." These little saints in the making are entrusted in the care of the Sunday schoolteacher, and they need the protection of the teacher's prayers. There is pressure on everyone in the Sunday school program, especially on those with some responsibility. Teachers are pivotal individuals in the program and should be diligent in praying for each student in the class. This is serious business, and God's protection and blessings are needed for all involved.

The position of DRE is a very responsible one and a very difficult one. Regulations from the diocese must be adhered to, the pastor needs to be informed regarding progress, and teachers and parents must be handled appropriately. There can be all sorts of stresses and strains on someone in this position. One of our DREs did a good job, but apparently got burned out and suddenly resigned. I was disappointed because she had been so effective.

One DRE was a very energetic, active person. She did many good things for the program, and I respected her authority. She was very conscious of connecting religious education to the rest of the parish. People in the parish need to be aware of our Sunday school efforts and to prayerfully support our program. She tried her best, but there were more distractions than usual, and it was difficult to maintain a consistent flow of class instruction.

The father is head of the family, according to Ephesians 5:23, and has responsibility for providing for and protecting the family. In the ideal family, the father should take primary responsibility for spiritual instruction of the children. Whoever resists God-appointed authority resists the ordinance of God, according to Romans 13:2. In many cases, however, men don't take their family religious responsibility seriously. The mother frequently becomes the center of spirituality in the family. Even if the father is a deeply spiritual person, the children are sometimes left to obtain their religious education from Sunday school or from church services. The mother and father are obviously important role models, but often they don't have time for formal religious instruction. Yet in Proverbs 22:6, it says, "train up a child in the way he should go and when he is old he will not depart from it." If we want our children to grow up to be responsible adults and good citizens, fathers need to take charge of the religious upbringing of their children. The Sunday school program should be supportive of the father's efforts.

Often fathers are too busy to even sit in on their children's Sunday school classes. Mostly, mothers come. When fathers do come however, they are generally very good and greatly strengthen the lessons being presented. Another believing, faith-filled male presence in the room has an amazingly powerful effect. Some fathers are very open and willing to reveal their deep convictions, and I am grateful for their help. I've made some good friendships with fathers who share my enthusiasm for Christ and who have helped with Sunday school classes.

I've had a few mothers attend my classes who seem skeptical and antagonistic. The students sense their attitude and tend to misbehave, and the lessons go poorly. This is rare since most mothers recognize the importance of CCD in the religious well-being of their children and are very helpful in class. We're all in this together.

Dr Elizabeth Blackwell, a Northwestern University psychologist, studied methods of training killer whales[8] and found they work in humans too. Animal trainers ignore silly and mischievous behavior and encourage only the behavior they want. It works. Dr Blackwell tried these methods at home on her husband and found they worked on him too. Also they work in Sunday school; I've tried it myself. It's sad to see Sunday schoolteachers correcting childish behavior in their students; it really does no good. But encouragement of desirable behavior with compliments or favors benefits the whole class.

The teacher is the authority in the classroom. Sometimes the children want to be in control (to be the general in command), and I've had parents come in and want to take charge. One parent came to class, assumed control, and started ordering me around. I didn't fight for control, but maybe I should have because the children misbehave when there is no distinct authority present. It's important to maintain that authority structure so that the instructional process can be conducted in an orderly manner.

In some of my classes, I have only twelve students, and it's difficult to arrange for parents to attend. We have a total of twenty-nine sessions per school year, and parents from each family need to come more than once. One time the parents of a young man had not made it for any of the classes, so, late in the spring, I invited them again. The mother said she'd come if she could bring her two-year-old with her. I was desperate so I said that would be OK. It was quite an experience. The mother brought the two-year-old who was excited about going to school. She sat next to her brother in the front row and busied herself with pencil and paper. When I began to speak to start the class, she made a hissing sound indicating she didn't want me to talk. She proceeded to flit between her brother and her mother who sat in the back of the room. All eyes were on her. She made the class laugh with all her antics, and I couldn't hold their attention as the little girl paraded back and forth in front of me. I didn't know what to do but instinctively reached down and picked her up and started to ask her questions about her family. This brought the

---

[8] "A Killer Whale of a Tale" by Elizabeth Corning Blackwell, Northwestern Alumni Magazine, Fall 2009

attention of the class back to me and sent a gentle message to the girl we had a class to conduct. This episode reinforced the idea that the teacher must maintain authority in the classroom in order for the lesson to be effective.

Two ways of maintaining order that I've used in the past are special seating and requesting students to leave the room. If two students (usually boys) interact excessively, I assign them seats some distance from one another. This is effective and well within the authority of the teacher, and most always works well. The other technique is to send the student who repeatedly disrupts the class out of the room. This is also usually effective. The student involved gets the point, and the rest of the class also comes to understand that being there is a privilege and they are to behave during class. When they leave the room, most students go out into the hall and simply stand by the door to the classroom. Usually they are somewhat embarrassed and stand there quietly. However, one student I had was a bright young man, very outspoken, and not very supportive of the purpose of the class. He had been told that he was exceptionally smart and was determined to show everyone that this was true. After several interruptions of the lesson in one class, I asked him to please leave the room. He obeyed, but as he stood outside, he made funny noises through the grating in the door and continued to disrupt the class. So asking the student who creates problems to leave the room doesn't always solve the difficulty.

In terms of chain of command, the teacher is the primary implement in each Sunday school class, but the DRE has primary working responsibility for the overall direction of the program. The whole process should aid the parents in their God-given task to train up a child in the way he or she should go.

Chapter 12

Westville Prison Visit

The important thing in life is to learn a lesson every time you lose.

—John McEnroe, American Tennis Champion

Please let me digress and tell about my experience in the prison ministry. It had an important impact on my involvement in the Sunday school program. Prior to going to Westville I never considered the prison ministry. Prisoners have made a mistake and are paying for it. Seems fair to me. Why trouble myself with the situation? But Matthew 25:36 says that we should visit those in prison.

Westville Correctional Center was established in 1977 on a 680 acre plot about eight miles west of Michigan City, IN. The facility was formerly a state mental institution. It currently houses about four thousand inmates and employs about one thousand guards. An organization known as "Kairos" ministers to Westville inmates twice each year, in May and November. The May 2007 visit was the sixth by our organization and was led by Charles Coleman of Indianapolis who had participated in the five previous Westville Prison visits by Kairos. Twenty-seven men from many different Christian churches in Indiana met several times to form friendships and to prepare for the May 2007 prison visit. We met at Westville Methodist Church Hall on Saturday mornings in March and April. This church was our base of operation for food preparation, housing, and meeting place to support our prison ministry.

Kairos Prison Ministry International grew out of the Catholic Cursillo movement which provides a short course in Christianity to revitalize local parishes. Kairos employs the same approach as Cursillo. Small "families" are formed (six inmates, two Kairos members, and one clergyman), and they share a table together. Each person takes notes and discusses all of the eleven talks that are presented. The talks examine (1) *self* (choices, you are not alone, friendship with God, the Church, opening the door), (2) *Christ* (discovery, action, being Christian), and (3) *others* (footprints in the sand, tomorrow, lighting the way). So each person is challenged to define where he is in relation to self, God, and others and to share what is in his heart with those in his "family." This is a proven renewal approach to revival of Christian Churches and started in Spain about sixty years ago. It encourages not only personal renewal, but also formation of deeply spiritual prayer groups and God-oriented relationships.

The Kairos Prison Ministry began in Florida in 1976. In 1979, the name "Kairos" was adopted, and the organization became incorporated as an independent, nonprofit, ecumenical Christian group approved by the Catholic Cursillo Secretariat, as well as by Presbyterian, Episcopal, Lutheran, United Methodist, Baptist, and other churches. Kairos is a Greek word meaning "God's special time" and is distinct from "chronos" a Greek word used for ordinary time. The time of the resurrection of Jesus would be referred to as Kairos. This prison ministry is a special time for God and reduces recidivism by 26-57 percent.

I was invited to participate in Kairos by a friend in one of my prayer groups. It involved six trips to Westville, IN (which is a ninety-minute drive from Lafayette) on Saturdays prior to the weekend prison visit. My last Sunday school class of the year was four days before we entered the prison.

There were thirty-six inmates enrolled in the program. They were screened by the prison chaplain and divided into six Kairos "families." Thursday evening we were fingerprinted and given volunteer worker passes, and we then met with the inmates. We each hosted one or two inmates and got acquainted with them. At 7:00 a.m. on Friday, we met our "families" (mine was the family of Luke) and began the program. Listen, listen, and love, love was our stated purpose. We patiently listened to stories of stabbings, noisy conditions (inmates purchase earplugs to sleep), and irritations like passing gas to annoy one another. We tried to bring the love of Christ into that environment.

We were told that food in the prison is generally unpalatable, and many inmates volunteer for our program because we bring special meals with fresh fruit. We purchased McDonald's double cheeseburgers and fries for one meal, and one of the inmates consumed seven double cheeseburgers, so starved was he for special foods. Also one inmate wept as he unwrapped his Big Mac. Some come for the food but get something much better.

We have an open microphone session on Saturday afternoons where inmates can say what they want. In previous Westville visits, only a few inmates spoke, but at our session all the inmates addressed the group. A miracle in itself. One young man told us he never felt real love in all his life before going through Kairos. All his life he had been put down and made to feel inferior, but now, for the first time, he knew that he was a worthwhile human being, loved by God and his fellow man. Through the tears he shared his powerful story. When he finished, he was greeted and hugged by many of his fellow inmates. This, mind you, occurred in a state penitentiary where that sort of behavior is not appropriate. You don't normally get a charismatic hug in the state pen!

As part of our ministry, we bring a dozen cookies to each of the four thousand inmates and one thousand guards at Westville. This is a huge undertaking. Parishioners in our churches and our Sunday school children prepare these "Kairos Kookies" and pray as they make them that God may reveal Himself to those in prison. The other Sunday schoolteachers as well as the parents in my CCD class are very helpful, and our church contributed 104 dozen cookies. Also our Sunday school children make placemats for the inmates with sayings like, "God loves you and He will never forsake you." Some inmates take these back to their cells and keep them. Of course, we also pray for the inmates in our Sunday school classes. It is amazing how God can get everyone involved in His work and enthused about His efforts to reach all His creation.

Immorality, dishonesty, suspicion, mistrust, and bad relationships abound in prisons. Twice our sessions had to be stopped so the guards could count the inmates to make sure no one had escaped. Inmates were frisked upon entering and leaving the gymnasium where the sessions were held. Satan does not appreciate Kairos, and we were warned of spiritual warfare prior to entry into the prison. One of our members went into the hospital about six weeks before we began to meet, and the doctors gave him no hope. Yet he recovered and made it through the weekend prison visit and was appreciated by the whole group. Our leader, Charles Coleman, was hospitalized the week before we entered Westville. He suffered from mental confusion and a very low heart rate. Yet he recovered and was very effective and proved to be a powerful guiding influence during the weekend. Although we ministered to only thirty-six out of four thousand inmates, the whole prison was talking about Kairos. The moral of the story is keep working for the Lord and He will sustain you, bless the work of your hands, and give you the victory.

There is no doubt in my mind that God wanted me at Westville. I was able to share some of the powerful stories I heard at my Kairos training sessions with my CCD class. They were good lessons for me and for my Sunday school students as well. Furthermore, the mothers of my students and all the other teachers who baked cookies contributed importantly to the prison mission. Their cookies and their many prayers were needed to support the efforts of Kairos to minister to the prison inmates.

Kairos Prison Ministry International Inc
- Grew out of Catholic Cursillo - same format
    - proven way for Church renewal
    - started in Spain about 60 years ago
    - groups ("families") of 9 people sit around tables and share thoughts/feelings about 11 different talks presented

Six training meetings were held at Methodist Church in Westville, IN in the weeks prior to entry into the prison. Purpose was to develop relationships between team members, to explain prison procedures and how Kairos witnesses to inmates.

Prison visit involved 27 men from many different Churches in Indiana Led by Charles Coleman (standing) from Indianapolis. Seated is Todd McCracken leader of the next prison visit being planned

Instructions
- how to dress
- no strong deodorant, aftershave
- don't ask why they're in prison
- nothing in, nothing out
- listen, listen; love, love

Another view of the Methodist Church in Westville. A Kairos trailer is shown which was used to transport food and equipment into the prison for use during our visit. Kairos Prison Ministry began in Florida in 1976; incorporated in 1979 as an ecumenical, independent, non-profit organization. Kairos is a Greek word meaning "God's special time"; differs from "chronos" which means ordinary time.

View from the outside of Westville Prison which is located on a 680 acre plot 8 miles west of Michigan City, IN. Pictured is Victor Cleveland, a fine Christian man, a former policeman from Frankfurt, IN. He gave the author a ride up to Westville for the prison visit.

One of the inmates drew a picture of the author freehand with a pencil and paper. They are generally talented, clever, intelligent people.

Chapter 13

Personal Benefits of Teaching Fourth Grade Sunday School

I love little children, and it is not a slight thing when they, who are fresh from God, love us.

—**Charles Dickens**

Probably the greatest blessing obtained from teaching fourth grade Sunday school is that you meet some really outstanding families. You see the love and the nurturing that goes into building those strong bonds and in forming those children into respectable citizens and responsible adults. In a way, the teacher becomes part of the family, someone who wants the best for them and helps in the vital formation process. When these parents are present, the classes seem to go better. They bring a measure of faith and goodwill to the classes which intensifies the spirituality and enhances the effectiveness of the lessons. Without the support and help of strong Christian families, there would be no quality Sunday school programs.

Seeing how God works in a Sunday school classroom is in itself a faith-building experience. Each student in my fourth grade Sunday school classes is asked to memorize the Twenty-third Psalm and then to recite it in front of the class. They have the whole school year to do this. These children are sharp and can do it easily. It only takes them about an hour to memorize it. Most children have no trouble, but one little boy made a great effort and still couldn't get it straight. His mother said he got all flustered when he tried to recite it and just couldn't do it. On the second-last session of the year, he told me before class that he was ready, and I was greatly pleased, especially because his mother was sitting in on the class that day. Then when I called on him to recite the Psalm he said he couldn't do it. I replied, "I thought you told me you were ready." He said that he did not know the Psalm. I was greatly disappointed, and I'm sure his mother was too. The boy himself must have been embarrassed also. I told him I wasn't going to force him and just went on with the class. The next week, however, the last session of the year, he mentioned again that he was ready to recite the Psalm. He did it beautifully. Praise God Who is our strength and help, as given in Psalm 46:1.

I'm in awe when I see how God arranges the Sunday school lessons and works in the lives of the students. It reminds me of Zechariah. He was a holy man of God, respected by his community, and served as a priest in the order of his division, according to Luke 1:8. His turn to take part in the services on the Sabbath was the opportunity for the angel to tell him about the birth of his son, John, to his barren wife, Elizabeth. Despite his basic belief in God, he had doubts about what the angel said. As a result, he was struck dumb. God had to get his attention before he could really understand the power and wonder of the Almighty. But then, nine months later when he wrote, "His name is John," he could speak again and uttered the profound words of "Zechariah's canticle." Good news for us all that we should be saved from our enemies and from the hand of all who hate us, that we might serve Him without fear, in holiness and righteousness before Him all the days of our life, as given in Luke 1:71-74. Zechariah had a deep, profound experience with the Holy Spirit and with the awesome power of God and spoke these good words from the depths of a believing heart. The Sunday schoolteacher likewise is given evidence of God's power and a deepening of faith. It is a great joy to witness the workings of the Holy Spirit in a fourth grade Sunday school class.

According to the book *I'm OK, You're OK*,[9] we each have three distinct personalities: a child who controls our behavior, e.g., when we play with the dog, we have an adult who is our logical self, and,

---

[9] Thomas A. Harris, *I'm OK, You're OK*, BBS Publishing Comp. New York, NY, 1967.

lastly, a parent. The child and parent are fully formed by the age of five years, but the adult continues to develop throughout life. An attractive personality has a healthy child to balance the adult and parent. The parental characteristics we have, we copy from our own parents, and although we may modify them a little with our own adult, they resemble those of our mothers and fathers. A good Sunday schoolteacher needs a healthy balance of all three personalities. I'm very grateful to my father and mother, although I can see where I have the same weaknesses and strengths that they had. My mother was the dominant parent and was responsible for most of the discipline. As the eldest child, I got more than my share of discipline, and I no doubt deserved it. But Mom also had a delightful child in her. When I was about four years old, my mother was making the beds one day, and as she flared out the covers onto the bed I dived under them. I did this several times so that she had to do it all over again. I know I was interfering with her work, but she recognized that I was playing a game and went along with it. I'm so appreciative that she didn't scold me and entered into my playful mood. Mom also had a very good "adult" personality, and I loved her deeply. She was a woman of great faith and made a strong effort to pass on her deep beliefs to her children. I'm forever grateful to her and must admit that what I do now is what I know pleases her and that includes teaching Sunday school.

My father was more laid back but a man of faith with a great ability to persevere in the face of difficulties. He was born in eastern Germany and came to the United Sates after World War I at the age of seventeen. Because of the war, there was a famine in Europe, and also schooling of children was disrupted. So my dad had only a few years of schooling and no higher education when he came to the United States, and he could not speak or write English at that time. Our family was poor because Dad worked at menial jobs all his life. I remember days when he was very sick and went in to work anyway. He was a good man and tried to be a good father. Once, after I had been involved in the Charismatic Movement (where hugs are freely given) for several years, I visited Dad, and on saying good-bye, I tried to give him a hug. However, that stiff German heritage came through, and it was a very awkward moment. Still, I love Dad and am grateful for having had such a fine father. Teaching Sunday school allows me to say a great big "thank you" to my mom and dad. Much of what I do on Sunday mornings reflects their goodness and enthusiasm for God.

I pray that what I do honors them and their faithfulness to the Lord, Jesus.

Teaching Sunday school allows me to see more clearly the need for God in everyone's life. The children need Him, the parents need Him, the pastor needs Him, and of course, the Sunday schoolteacher needs Him as well. For our communities and nations to function well, people need to be guided by the Holy Spirit and become people of forgiveness, compassion, and love. This is true on a national level as well as on a personal one. I recognize the necessity and value of the military, but I'm grateful for the peacefulness we have had so that neither of my sons had to go to war. The movie *Saving Private Ryan* illustrates the chaos, futility, and absolute evil of war. A Vietnam veteran recently made the statement that it would have been more beneficial if they had sent young men over there with Bibles instead of rifles. The whole world would have been much better off. When a godly attitude pervades a society, there is peace and goodness. As it says in Psalm 133:1, "How good and how pleasant it is for brethren to dwell together in unity." I am speaking to you as someone who has served in the U.S. Army Medical Service Corps and was honorably discharged with the rank of Captain.

After one of my classes, one of the parents came up to me and mentioned that she didn't know how people function without having God as the center of their lives. I immediately agreed with her and said it's a great mystery to me also. Probably it reflects God's great mercy and love for all those He created. It's a great honor and privilege as a Sunday schoolteacher to point out the emptiness within the soul of mankind and the requirement to fill that void with love and reverence for God as reflected by a holy life.

Chapter 14

Conclusion

To experience Jesus' love for me is the greatest consolation I could have on this earth. How eager I should be to share it with others.

—Monsignor David E. Rosage, Retreat Center Director, Spokane, Washington.

In one of our Sunday school meetings, a question was asked whether the teacher should have a movie for each class. The answer given was that a good movie or filmstrip should be shown in every class, and each class should have a clear, effective lesson to be taught. This is serious business, and we need to make efficient use of each class meeting and at the same time make the experience enjoyable for all.

Sunday school is indeed God's special time, a Kairos event. Just as in the Kairos Prison Ministry, God reaches out to His lost sheep and tries to bring them back into the fold to give them that joy and peace He promised, so we must reach out and gather in the lambs who come to us in Sunday school.

Victor Frankel, a psychiatrist and survivor of the Nazi prison camp, Auschwitz, wrote, "To live is to suffer, and to endure is to find meaning in suffering." Teaching Sunday school is not exactly suffering, but it is not always easy either, and it takes an effort. However, the need is clear, and the goodness is obvious. I'm sure it was an effort for Jesus to perform His ministry also, but He didn't constantly complain about the difficulties. He had a purpose-driven life, and it was a pleasure and an honor for Him to serve His Father.

As Chuck Colson points out,[10] throughout their history, Christians have acted contrary to society. Instead of hating our enemies, we forgive and try to do good for all. We have a preference for the poor and downtrodden, establishing hospitals and orphanages and providing food and shelter for the needy. We operate on a fundamentally different level and have found a superior "life force" that sustains us. We know that we are empowered from above by the Holy Spirit. Much of the good accomplished in this world is done not by governments, but by Christians inspired by the Holy Spirit.

Often Christians find themselves in opposition to the government. Deitrich Bahnhoffer knew the German government of his day was evil and lost his life in April 1944 trying to rectify the situation. From the time of the Roman Empire to the present day in all parts of the world, governments have persecuted Christians. Christians have responded in love and generosity and still today continue their humanitarian efforts. Children in Sunday school need to be made aware of this great struggle, and hopefully they are being prepared to join in the battle.

May I digress briefly to make an important point? People must work for justice to have peace. The peace treaty at Versailles after World War I was unjust, grossly unfair, and practically mandated World War II. Another war was almost inevitable because of the revenge and retribution, which were the basis of the provisions of the Versailles "peace treaty". The French especially had experienced destruction and terror at the hands of the German military. They were out to get even, to force the Germans to pay for the anguish they caused, and to prevent any further problems. The treaty required Germany to pay a staggering amount of money and to relinquish much of its territory. There was no appeal or negotiation allowed for the Germans. The whole thing was ludicrous, and thus seeds of World War II were planted. We all need a strong sense of justice in order to promote peace. (Evil men do not understand justice, but those who seek the Lord understand all, according to Proverbs 28:5.) This important lesson should not be forgotten and should be emphasized in our Sunday school classes.

Despite the unfairness of the Versailles peace treaty, the Germans did not have to respond with war. Germany was a Christian nation, with an even mix of Lutherans and Catholics. Hitler was a Catholic. Why did

---

[10] Chuck Colson, *The Faith,* Zondervan, Grand Rapids, MI, 2009.

the German people and the German Government depart from Christian principles and permit the invasion of Poland in August 1939? Probably because we all tend to do things our own way and not God's way. We're all too human and do what we think is right ("For as high as the heavens are above the earth, so high are my ways above your ways." (Isa. 55:9). But also maybe our churches are not strong enough, and perhaps our Sunday school programs don't fully reflect the Good News which Jesus Christ has given to us.

The deep problems we now have with liberal or atheistic governments throughout the world challenge us as nations and as individuals to adopt more ethical standards to respect all forms of life. As Pope John Paul II said, "Nations that destroy their own children cannot survive." May God forgive us and have mercy on us and lead us back to virtue.

The key central event in the history of mankind was the resurrection of Jesus Christ. Because He rose from the dead, we can believe the words of Holy Scripture; we can believe in eternal life, and there is hope for all people. All the great advances made by men and women pale into insignificance by comparison. We think air travel, computers, modern medicine, and fine automobiles are so magnificent. Yet they are of no value for eternity. All these things will pass away. The sun will burn out, and things of earth will cease to exist. As Jesus said, "Heaven and earth will pass away but my words will not pass away" (Mark 13:31). What could be more important than teaching young children to love and respect their Creator?

www.ingramcontent.com/pod-product-compliance
Lightning Source LLC
Chambersburg PA
CBHW060342080526
44584CB00013B/889